Mrs Lewis

Wools and how to use them

Mrs Lewis

Wools and how to use them

ISBN/EAN: 9783742832023

Manufactured in Europe, USA, Canada, Australia, Japa

Cover: Foto ©Lupo / pixelio.de

Manufactured and distributed by brebook publishing software
(www.brebook.com)

Mrs Lewis

Wools and how to use them

BERLIN HOUSE

JEVONS & MELLOR,

Wool Importers and Merchants,

BERLIN HOUSE,

CORPORATION STREET AND OLD SQUARE,

BIRMINGHAM.

WOOLS

HOW TO USE THEM

BY

MRS. LEWIS,

Meopham Vicarage,
Kent.

AUTHOR OF "DIRECTIONS FOR KNITTING SOCKS AND
STOCKINGS," "THE MEOPHAM SAMPLER," "DOMESTIC SERVICE
IN THE PRESENT DAY," ETC.

———

— Price One Shilling. —

———

SECOND EDITION.

PUBLISHED BY JEVONS AND MELLOR,
BIRMINGHAM.

Hudson and Son, Printers, Edmund Street, Birmingham.

CONTENTS.

CHAPTER I.

CONCERNING WOOLS.

All workers, especially those whose work requires wool, yarn, etc., must be struck with the great advance which has been made in the last 25 years in the manufacture of these articles.

In former days we had double and single Berlin—the latter in tiny skeins—Fleecy of a very inferior quality and a few makes of yarn—these latter were, for the most part, harsh, heavy in weight, and liable to shrink, with only a few colours, and all were very expensive.

Under such adverse circumstances we cannot wonder that, in those days, women devoted themselves more to sewing and did no knitting and only a little crochet shawl or something of that sort now and then by way of a treat, all the time regarding it as an expensive amusement which could only be indulged in on rare occasions and with apologies.

Far be it from me to discourage plain sewing, being myself a warm advocate of the art, I look upon it as a thoroughly feminine accomplishment with great scope for skill, a means of educating the eye and hand, and quite sure to be useful to every woman in the land, whether noble lady or lowly maiden; but the perfection of the sewing machine has relieved woman of a vast amount of the drudgery, no more interminable seams to be sewn, no more tedious stitching, and thus a

clever worker has a great deal more time at her
disposal, which she can employ pleasantly to herself
and profitably to her family by knitting, to say nothing
of other work—and here I would observe that really
good plain sewing is an admirable training for other
work—in fact I do not believe that excellence can be
obtained without it; and I am quite sure that, to
succeed in other work, a good foundation must have
been laid in this manner.

The better we work the more we shall like it and
whatever we undertake, if wo do our very best, we
shall find a double reward, that of producing a really
good article, and the pleasure of the work itself.

There have been many books of instruction for the
Knitter, the Crochet Worker, the Embroiderer, etc.,
and these did good service, but they gave as a rule
little information as to wool and that little related to
the wools then obtainable. It seems to me, therefore,
that the time has come when a little book which should
treat of wools and give instructions for using them,
would be useful and welcome, especially if brought
down to the present date.

I propose, therefore, to give a list of wools of reliable
make, wools which I can recommend from practical
acquaintance as combining the several points which
are essential, viz., lightness, strength, softness, not
liable to shrink, fast colour and moderate price; and
to add instructions for a great many useful articles
which can be made with them.

My chief aim has been to give recipes which would
be useful to ordinary knitters, nothing very elaborate,
but great care has been taken to render them as simple
as possible, each one has been tested, and if the instructions be followed implicitly, they will be found quite
easy and perfectly correct.

PREFACE TO SECOND EDITION.

In preparing another edition of this little book I have revised it very carefully, and made such alterations as have seemed desirable. I have given a fuller description of the wools mentioned therein, and hope that all knitters, especially the inexperienced, for whom chiefly it is intended, will find all they require within its pages. At the end of instructions for sock knitting (page 18), will be found remarks about knitting needles, but it is so important, and so seldom grasped, that I think I must put it before my readers more prominently. It very often happens that a knitter follows a recipe, carefully using the wool recommended and the same number needles, when the article is finished she is disappointed to find that it comes out larger or smaller than she expected ; because she is a tight or loose knitter, and the needles were not suitable to her particular work. Then again, some inexperienced knitters will use a much coarser wool, and any needles they have—perhaps not all the same size—and are surprised that the work turns out badly. Knitting requires good wool, i.e., wool suitable for the purpose, and good needles. I have given the sizes for medium knitters, but it is *quite impossible* to lay down a hard and fast rule for needles, you can only learn by experience. If quite a beginner, make a pair of socks exactly according to instructions, and when you see how it turns out you can judge for the future. If any difficulty should arise I shall be happy to answer any lady, provided she encloses an addressed stamped envelope. See address on fly leaf.

8

The "Table" will be found extremely useful.

List of wools mentioned in this book, all to be obtained from Messrs. Jevons and Mellor, Corporation Street, Birmingham.

For socks and stockings, beginning with the coarsest and ending with the finest—excellent ranges of colour—it should always be borne in mind that fancy mixtures and bright colours are rather more expensive than heathers, greys, &c., the quality is of course the same.

Alloa, for shooting hose and Deep Sea Mission.

Scotch Fingerings, No. 1, strong and coarse.

        ,,   No. 2, ditto but finer.

        ,,   No. 3, strong, but softer and less coarse.

        ,,   No. 4, strong, but softer and fuller.

        ,,   No. 4½, strong, but finer and softer still.

Sicilian, 8-fold, strong and thick, yet soft for superior knitting.

      ,,   6-fold, the same but finer.

      ,,   4-fold, beautifully soft and fine.

Bee-hive, a soft fine wool.

Rutland, very fine, for best hosiery.

Zephyr, fleecy.

Extra super fleecy.

Super fleecy.

Petticoat yarn.

German Fingering, No. 8.

      ,,   No. 7.

      ,,   No. 6.

Worcester yarn.

Berlin, 8-fold.

   ,,   4-fold.

Berlin Fingerings.

Shawl wool.

Indian cashmere.

New Crochet wool, has a beautiful twist, which is
very effective.

Dame wool.

Eider.

Andalusian.

Natural colour wool, 6 and 4-fold.

Vest wool, 4.fold and 2-fold.

Madras yarn, with an admixture of silk, old Indian
colours, which have an excellent effect.

Lady Betty, 4, 3, and 2-ply, white only.

Coral wool, fine, prettily twisted.

Ostrich wool, a silky appearance, forming natural
rings.

Rabbit, thick fluffy wool.

Shetland, winter.

     ,,   summer.

Ice wool, very fine and silky.

Pyrenees wool, extremely fine.

Prices of all the above qualities on application to

Messrs. JEVONS AND MELLOR, Corporation Street,
Birmingham.

TABLE FOR KNITTING SOCKS AND STOCKINGS.

	Boys' Socks				Men's Socks			Stockings						
Size	1	2	3	4	4	6	0	1	2	3	4	5	6	7
Cast on 1st Needle	30	24	24	28	28	28	36	24	28	32	36	38	38	40
" 2nd "	17	21	25	28	28	28	32	24	25	29	33	33	37	40
" 3rd "	34	38	42	51	40	40	54	73	81	89	97	105	113	121
Total	67	65	73	81	40	60	97	73	81	89	97	105	113	121
Ribbed in twos	34	38	42	40	60	50	54	20	20	20	22	24	26	28
Plain Rounds	20	22	24	26	30	34	34	100	104	108	112	110	120	128
Mark the size in seventh round of all sizes.														
Leg decreasings	2	2	2	2	3	3	7	10	11	12	13	14	15	10
Rows between	1	7	7	7	7	7	7	7	7	7	7	7	7	7
Number of Stitches	63	61	67	75	83	89	89	63	69	65	71	77	83	89
Plain Rounds	12	10	20	24	21	28	28	28	30	30	40	46	50	55
Divide for Heel, Front Stitches	26	31	34	38	43	41	44	25	33	33	35	38	42	44
Back Stitches	27	31	33	37	36	38	45	27	33	33	36	34	34	45
Rows in " Straight Piece "	22	24	28	32	32	16	38	22	24	28	30	32	19	30
Heel Stitches	9	9	13	15	16	21	19	9	13	13	15	17	19	21
Stitches to pick up each side of Straight Piece	13	15	17	19	19	23	23	13	17	17	19	21	23	25
Number of Stitches, 1st Needle	17	20	23	26	29	29	32	17	20	23	28	29	33	30
" " 2nd "	26	30	34	34	34	43	44	25	30	33	35	38	42	44
" " 3rd "	18	21	24	37	37	21	33	18	24	24	30	30	33	35
Total	61	71	81	91	91	101	109	61	71	70	89	97	107	116
Heel Decreasings	1	1	2	2	2	2	2	1	3	3	2	2	2	2
Side Decreasings	3	7	6	6	7	7	8	3	6	6	7	8	10	11
Number Stitches	63	61	67	73	83	83	89	63	63	65	71	77	83	89
Plain rounds in Foot	36	40	44	48	48	56	56	36	42	44	46	48	50	52
Toe Decreasings	8	9	10	11	11	12	13	9	10	10	11	12	13	14
Number of Stitches to Finish	21	25	27	31	31	35	37	17	19	25	27	29	31	33

CHAPTER II.

SOCKS AND STOCKINGS.

The first ambition of a knitter is to knit stockings, and when we consider how easy it is, how economical, and how fascinating an employment, we can only wonder that every woman is not a knitter. However busy she may be there are always odd moments in which the knitting, if ready to hand, can be taken up—no thimble, scissors, cotton, etc., to be found—but everything ready ; it does not require keen sight nor much attention, and is the only work exactly suitable for the employment of those spare minutes (some of us have so many in the day) which would otherwise be wasted.

Knitting does not require much thought, and is therefore excellent for those women whose minds are occupied with weighty matters which they can think about as well, or even better, while their fingers are employed.

GENTLEMEN'S SOCKS (Medium Size.)

No. 5 on Table.

Materials required 4 oz. Sicilian Wool, 6-fold, 4 short steel knitting needles, No. 15, or, if a loose knitter, No. 16.

12

Cast on 32 stitches on 1st needle, 28 stitches on the 2nd needle, and 29 on the 3rd needle, making a total of 89 stitches—the odd stitch is for the seam stitch, and is the last stitch of the round. The seam stitch it very important indeed; all calculations are made from it, therefore it must never be overlooked —some knitters purl the seam stitch in every row— but I think it looks better to be knitted and purled alternately, and it certainly is more easy to count.

Rib in twos for 50 rounds, keeping the seam stitch.

30 plain rounds—in the 7th of these mark the size, thus—knit 6 plain stitches, then put the wool forward and knit two together—do this five times for this size, which is No. 5; five small holes will appear. In the second sock knit round to within thirteen of the seam stitch, then wool forward, knit two together five times, then 6 plain and seam stitch; it will be observed that on one sock the size mark is done on the 1st needle; in the second sock it is done on the 3rd needle in order that it may appear on the outside of both socks

When the 30 plain rounds are done we begin to decrease in the leg.

2 plain stitches knit two together, knit round plain to within 4 of seam—knit two together 2 plain, seam —note that the decreasings are each side of the seam and that there are 2 plain stitches between the decrease and the seam stitch.

7 plain rows.

Decrease again as before.

7 plain rounds.

Decrease again.

There should now be 83 stitches on the needles. 26 plain rounds (and seam).

Divide for the heel, 41 stitches will be required, knit to twenty past seam—put the remaining stitches on the 2nd needle, turn, purl back these 20, seam, purl 20 from the 3rd needle, put the remaining stitches on to the 2nd needle. There should now be 42 stitches on the 2nd or instep needle, and 41 on the 1st and 3rd needles, then for greater convenience of working put the instep stitches on two needles and have the 41 back stitches on 1st needle—be quite sure that the seam stitch is exactly in the middle— i.e., that there are 20 stitches on each side of it.

Knit and purl backwards and forwards on these 41 stitches, for 36 rows, the 1st stitch must be slipped and the wool kept tight in order to make a neat firm edge, along which we shall presently have to pick up stitches, leave off with a purled row.

Put the instep stitches on one needle, knit to 4 past seam, wool forward, slip 1, wool back, turn (in this part of the sock the 1st stitch is not to be slipped, the reason being obvious, it was slipped before and must be knitted or purled now.)

Purl to 4 past seam, wool back, slip 1, wool forward, turn.

Knit to 5 past seam, wool forward, slip 1, wool back, turn.

Purl to 5 past seam, wool back, slip 1, wool forward, turn.

Repeat these 2 rows, knitting 1 stitch further each time (making the purled row the same number of stitches as the previous knitted one) till there are 8 stitches each side of the seam, 17 in all, these are called "heel stitches" and are thus designated in the table which will be found at the end of this chapter.

Having now 17 stitches in the centre of the heel needle, and 8 each side of seam, and the wool at the last slipped stitch, turn, knit to 7 past seam and take 2 together, now the 1st stitch is to be slipped henceforth.

Purl back to 7 past seam, purl 2 together, turn, continue these 2 rows till all the stitches are taken up on each side and there are only the 17 heel stitches on the needle—finish with a purled row—knit along the 17 stitches, discontinue the seam, pick up 21 stitches along the side of the "straight piece;" these must be knitted, for the appearance of the work and in order to have the wool ready for the instep needle.

Knit the 42 instep stitches, knit up 21 stitches along the other side of the "straight piece," and knit 9 stitches off the 1st needle on to the 3rd.

There should now be 101 stitches altogether; on the 1st needle 29, 2nd needle 42, 3rd needle 30, the last stitch comes exactly in the centre of the sole of the foot where the seam stitch was.

We shall presently make a seam stitch each side of the foot instead.

Having completed the heel and picked up the side stitches, and having satisfied ourselves that we have the right number on each needle individually, we proceed to the foot.

Knit 2 plain rounds.

3rd round.

1st needle, 2 together, knit 22, 2 together, 2 plain, 1 purl.

2nd needle, plain.

3rd needle, 1 purl, 2 plain, knit 2 together, 22 plain, 2 together, 1 plain.

Note that the 2 purl stitches are for the new seam stitches along each side of the foot, the last stitch of 1st needle and 1st stitch of 3rd needle are to be knitted and purled alternately till the beginning of the toe, the decreasing before the 1st and after the 2nd seam are called the "side decreasings," those close to the heel are called "heel decreasings." 4 stitches less in the round, 2 plain rounds (keeping side seams).

6th round, heel and side decreasings as before.

2 plain rounds.

9th round. 1st needle ; knit till there are only 5 stitches left on the needle, 2 together, 2 plain, seam.

2nd needle, plain.

3rd needle, seam stitch, 2 plain, 2 together, plain, to end of needle.

2 plain rounds.

12th round, same as 9th.

2 plain rounds.

15th same as 9th.

Continue the side decreasings with 2 plain rounds between till you have made 7 decreasings each side beside those at the heel.

There should now be 83 stitches on the needles—the same number that we had when we divided for the heel—it is an invariable rule that when we begin the plain rounds for the foot, there should be the same number of stitches as when we had completed the last leg decrease. For the foot 50 plain rounds, keeping side seams all the time.

For the toe : 1st needle, knit till there are 4 stitches left, knit 2 together, 2 plain ; henceforth the side seams are discontinued.

2nd needle : 2 plain, 2 together, knit till there are 4 stitches left at end of needle, 2 together, 2 plain.

3rd needle : 2 plain, 2 together, plain to end of needle.

It will be perceived that the decrease takes place 4 times in the round and is referred to in the table as a toe decrease.

3 plain rounds.

5th round, toe decrease (4 times in round).

3 plain rounds.

9th round, toe decrease.

2 plain rounds.

12th   toe decrease.
2 plain rounds.
15th   toe decrease.
1 plain round.
17th   toe decrease.

Continue these two last rounds alternately till there are only 35 stitches left, there should be 12 toe decreasings of 4 stitches each.

Knit to the end of 1st needle, turn the sock on the wrong side, which can be done quite easily through the opening at the toe—put the back stitches on one needle and cast off from the two needles at once—the extra stitch must be got rid of by knitting 2 together in centre of needle—fasten off the ends neatly.

In the "Table" three sizes of Boys' and three of Men's Socks are given, these will be found sufficient for all ordinary knitters, these sizes can again be varied by using finer or coarser wool and smaller or larger needles.

The instructions given will be found a very useful size ; the knitter is advised to make a pair following those instructions implicitly, she will then be able to judge the other sizes from it.

If silk socks be required, No. 6 size and 16 needles, 2 ozs. silk—some knitters knit the 50 ribbed rows in Andalusian wool, to avoid their slipping down, which silk is apt to do, and it lessens the expense, but the wool and silk must match exactly.

For schoolboys, where great strength is required, Alloa or Scotch Fingering No. 4 are admirable, and there is a wide range of colour—but it should be borne in mind that it is heavier than the better qualities, and there are 50 instead of 60 rounds to the oz.—consequently more will be required. 4ozs. is plenty for boys' socks.

For stockings proceed in exactly the same way as
for socks, referring to the "table."

For ladies' stockings medium size, No. 5 on the
scale, 4-fold Sicilian or Rutland—6oz. needles No. 16.
If thinner stockings be required Andalusian and 16
needles—No. 6 size on the "table." For silk stockings No. 7 size 17 needles—4ozs. silk.

If the socks or stockings are to be ribbed, rib in
twos for the number of rounds indicated in the
"table," then rib with 3 plain 1 purl or 7 plain 1 purl;
discontinue the ribbing at the sole of the foot and on
all three needles when you begin the toe decreasings.

To thicken the heel, knit in Shetland wool, beginning
at the straight piece; for the toe, begin to thicken at
the 1st toe decrease.

The foregoing is the easiest way of thickening a
heel, but it is not the way required by the education
code. To thicken a heel, work as follows: Divide for
the heel as already directed, and in every *knitted* row
slip each alternate stitch, purl the row back as usual,
you will perceive that the slipping is only done in the
"straight" piece, in the knitted rows only. Knitting
in this way seems to contract the work, so if you
decide to knit a thickened heel you should make the
"straight" piece 4 or 6 rows longer than the "table"
directs.

There are various heels in use among knitters; the
one here recommended the "Dutch heel," is the
one generally preferred from its strength and good fit,
and is the one required by the Educational Code in
Elementary schools.

To refoot socks and stockings, cut off the worn part
at the ankle where the stitches were divided for the
"straight piece"—unravel the wool till the stitches
are perfect and pick them up on three needles—if the
size has been marked, the knitter can go on at once

by the " table "—if not, the stitches must be counted
at the foot and worked accordingly.

If the knitter has always been in the habit of using
the same make of wool she can always match it for
refooting.

The legs will always wear out two pairs of feet,
and it is most satisfactory to have virtually new socks
at half the cost and half the work.

It takes nearly 2ozs. to refoot socks or stockings.

N.B —It should be distinctly understood that in
specifying sizes of needles it is impossible to lay down
any hard and fast rule ; no two people knit alike ;
and numbers can therefore only be given as a guide—
the knitter will soon learn by experience the sizes
which suit her work best.

CHAPTER III.

FLEECY AND PETTICOAT YARN.

In no class of wool is the improvement more striking than in Fleecy and Petticoat Fingerings. In former days Fleecy was never used except for very common purposes and Petticoat Fingering was unknown. Now they are so good that they can be used with advantage in place of Double Berlin, and for some purposes they are preferable ; there is a lightness and softness about them which is quite beautiful, and in the following articles either can be used to advantage.

Fleecy is brought to such perfection now that it may be used for working cushions, kneelers, etc. for Churches. All the proper ecclesiastical colours can be had, it is less expensive than double Berlin—and where large quantities are required and economy an object, Fleecy can be used perfectly well—and I do not think there are many people who would know the difference.

In the following recipes the knitting is almost entirely done backwards and forwards on two needles ; it should be borne in mind therefore that it is an invariable rule to slip the 1st stitch of every row, and keep the wool quite tight, this will ensure a firm even edge which is equally necessary both to the appearance and the durability of the work, and it is to be done *always* unless expressly stated to the contrary.

1. KNEE CAPS.

4 ozs. Fleecy or Petticoat or Allon, or Scotch Fingerings, No. 2 or 4.

Colour—white, scarlet or natural colour. 1 pair of
bone or wooden needles, No. 8. Cast on 50 stitches.

Knit backwards and forwards for 12 rows. In the
13th row increase in the 25th stitch by making a
stitch in the back of the work (this is to avoid a hole),
knit plain to the end of the row.

Increase in the 25th stitch of every row till there
are 75 stitches, then knit 24 plain rows.

In the next row, 24 plain stitches, knit 2 together,
plain to the end of the row.

Decrease thus in every row till there are 50 stitches
on the needle, then knit 12 plain rows and cast off.

When both knee caps are knitted sew them up with
a wool needle, taking the "cast on" and "cast off"
edges together, stitch by stitch, fasten off the ends
securely.

2. TENNIS CAP (Crochet.)

These caps are very simple, quickly made and are
generally found to sell extremely well at bazaars.

3 ozs. Petticoat Fingering, or Fleecy or Shawl
Wool (crimson, navy blue or other colour); coarse
steel crochet needle. It should be worked tight so as
to give firmness to the work.

For the crown make a loop of wool and into it work
4 D.C. stitches.

Begin each round with 2 chain and end with a
single stitch in the 2nd of the 2 chain, this is to
complete the round.

Each round must be complete before the next is
begun; increase as often as is necessary to form a flat
crown, perfectly round; when it measures 7½ inches

across, begin the band, continue working round and round in the same way without any increase for 2½ inches and then work single stitches in the last round to give strength and firmness to the edge; fasten off the ends, and line the cap with crimson or navy blue silk, or twill as circumstances may suggest.

If this cap be worked firmly and evenly in accordance with the instructions it will be found very satisfactory.

3. WARM SCARF.

4ozs. White Fleecy or Petticoat Yarn, or coloured, 2 wooden needles No. 3.

Cast on 23 stitches and knit 1 plain row.

1st row.   3 plain, wool forward, knit 2 together, till there are only 2 stitches left on the needle —knit these plain.

2nd row.   3 plain, wool forward, 2 together—finish with 2 plain.

Begin each row with 3 plain and finish with 2 plain; all the rest is putting the wool forward and taking 2 together.

When the scarf is long enough, finish the ends with fringe of the same wool; which can be looped in with a crochet needle; or the two edges can be folded in the middle and the ends finished with a tassel.

4. GAUNTLETS (Men's).

These also are excellent things to make for Bazaars, the outlay is small, they are not difficult, and always find a ready sale.

3ozs. Petticoat Fingering or 8-fold Berlin (black or crimson), 4 steel needles, No. 12 for a loose knitter, No. 11 for a tight knitter.

These gauntlets are knitted backwards and forwards on two needles, the extra needles are required for the thumbs.

Cast on (tight) 50 stitches and knit a plain row.

First row : knit 30, purl 20.

Second and third rows : plain.

Fourth row : purl 20, knit 30.

Fifth and sixth : plain.

Repeat from first row till there are 10 ribs on each side of the work, i.e., 60 rows in all.

The ribbed part is for the wrist, the plain part for the hand.

The edge, top and bottom, must have been kept firm and regular and even, by means of the slipped stitch, which is of great importance, in all 2 needles knitting—but in gauntlets it is absolutely essential.

Having completed the 10 ribs on each side, or 60 rows, leave off with the wool at the top of the muffatee (not at the wrist), and begin the thumb.

Knit 7 stitches down and leave them ; take another needle and with it cast on 7 stitches on the 1st needle, to replace the 7 which have just been knitted off so as to have 50 stitches.

Knit 28 stitches and turn, leaving 22 stitches (including the ribbing) to themselves for the present.

Take the 4th needle, slip 1st stitch, take 2 together, plain to the end.

Knit back plain and turn.

Slip 1st stitch, 2 together, plain to end, turn.

Knit back plain.

It will be perceived that in every alternate row there is a reduction of 1 stitch which is made at the bottom of the thumb.

Continue these two rows until there are only 8 stitches left on the needle.

Leave off with the wool at the top of the thumb.

Cast off 7 stitches, leaving 1 stitch on the needle ;

with that needle knit 20 stitches along the slanting
edge of the thumb, inserting the needle between the
rows; then knit the 22 stitches which have been left
untouched so long, *i.e.*, to the end of the ribbing turn.

Purl 20 and knit 23, which should bring the knitter
to end of the needle, then knit off the 7 stitches which
were left when the thumb was commenced.

There should now be only the 2 original needles in
use and 50 stitches; continue ribbing and plain till
the gauntlet is large enough, 15 or 16 ribs in all.

Be careful to have the same number of ribs on both
sides of the work that they may join properly.

Cast off (loosely) and sew the 2 edges together
carefully stitch by stitch with the wool, also the
thumb.

This gauntlet is for the right hand.

For the left proceed exactly in the same way till
the 10 ribs are completed and the 7 stitches cast on
for the thumb; but make your reduction as you go
down the thumb, knitting 2 together in the last stitch
but 1.

Make the plain row as you come up.

When the thumb is finished cast off 7 stitches and
turn the gauntlet for the left hand, and in taking up
the stitches along the slanting edge of the thumb purl
them instead of knitting them. All the rest is the
same.

For a smaller size, cast on 40 stitches, 25 plain, 15
purl; 8 ribs on each side. To commence the thumb
knit off 5 stitches, cast on 5.

Knit down to within 2 stitches of the ribs, 4 ribs
after the thumb.

2 ozs. wool ample for this size.

In all cases the seam must come in the palm of the
hand.

5. BEDROOM SLIPPERS (Lady's Size.)

Materials required ; Fleecy or Petticoat Fingering.
3 ozs. crimson, 2 ozs. white, grey, or stone.
1 pair of cork soles, No. 4.
1 yard of braid or ribbon to bind the soles.
4 steel needles, No. 12.

These slippers are knitted backwards and forwards
on 2 needles and a firm even edge is highly
important.

With the dark wool cast on 17 stitches and knit 4
plain rows.

5th row ; 1 plain, take the light wool insert the
right hand needle in the next stitch and make a loop
over the finger and needle, but *knit* the stitch with
the dark wool—1 plain, loop with light wool—after
the 1st, the loop is made by passing the wool under
the first finger and over the needle from back to
front, knit with the dark wool and always keep the
dark wool above the light, repeat to end of row, every
other stitch having a loop, cut the light wool.

6th, knit back plain.

7th, row with loops.

8th, knit back plain.

9th, plain, increase in the last stitch but one by
making a stitch in the back of work.

10, 11 and 12 the same as 9.

Repeat these last 8 rows 5 times more ; this is for
the front of the slipper and there should be 41 stitches
on the needle.

For the sides and back.

Knit 15 stitches (with loops of light wool) and
leave 26 on the needle ; take another needle, and knit
back plain along the 15 stitches, then a looped
row, then 5 plain rows exactly the same as the toe
without increasings ; continue this straight piece of

15 stitches till it is long enough to fit the sole, 17 or 18 rows (double) of loops will be required, leave off with the wool at the outer edge, cast off these 15 stitches with 15 of those at the toe, and then cast off the 11 centre stitches, be careful to cast off on the wrong, or looped side of the work. Knit thus far with both slippers. Bind the soles with ribbon or braid to match and sew on the knitted part; they should be sewn with the loops outside and then turn the slipper right side out.

The worker should be careful to preserve the shape of the slipper, and strength and neatness are very important.

To make a ruche for the top cast on with the dark wool 5 stitches. 1 plain, 3 with loops of wool which must be passed over the finger and needle two or three times according to the thickness required, 1 plain, knit back plain.

6 rows of each colour, i.e.; 3 looped and 3 plain rows, or it can be made of one colour only; continue till the ruche is long enough, cast off and sew up.

Sew on the ruche.

These slippers are very suitable for gentlemen, but for the ruche a roll round the top must be substituted, and a larger size required.

Cast on 21, continue the front till there are 51 stitches, 17 stitches along the side, 17 left when the slipper is joined up. These 17 are not to be cast off, pick up stitches all round the top of the slipper with two more needles and with the 4th knit round and round rather tight for 7 or 8 rounds, then cast off, and fasten the ends—this will form a thick firm roll and does not take so much wool as the ruche—therefore, for man's size 4oz. dark, and 1oz light wool will be sufficient.

6.   BASSINET BLANKET, Double Knitting.

Materials required : 2 long wooden needles No. 7,
1lb. Fleecy or Petticoat, white or scarlet ; cast on
90 stitches, knit as loosely as possible, but of course
evenly.

Slip 1st stitch of every row.

2 plain, put the wool in front of needle, slip 1, wool
back, knit 1, wool forward, slip 1, wool back, knit 1,
—continue till there are only three stitches left on
needle which must invariably be knitted ; in double
knitting the rule is that the stitch which is slipped in
one row is knitted in the next.   End with a plain
row before casting off.

If preferred a wider edge can be made by putting
more plain stitches at the beginning and end of each
row of the blanket.   A coloured edge may be knitted
and sewn on after if required.

7.   SOFA BLANKET, Brioche Stitch.

This is knitted in stripes, and the colours arranged
according to the taste of the worker.   Allow ¼lb.
Fleecy or 8-fold Berlin for each stripe ; of which
there will be sufficient for fringe or tassels at the ends.

2 wooden needles No. 4.

Knit loosely ; slip 1st stitch of every row and keep
the edge firm, even and tight.

Cast on 22 stitches and knit 1 row.

2 plain wool forward. slip 1, knit 2 together, repeat
till there are only two stitches left on the needle which
are to be knitted—every row is exactly the same ;
always begin and end with 2 plain—take care that in
each row the slipped stitch is the one where 2 were
knitted together in the previous row.

The stripes should be crocheted or sewn together
with some bright colour and the ends finished with
fringe or tassels, the sides should be left plain.

Brioche stitch is most useful for a variety of purposes, we shall use it again for an infant's hood, and the knitter will do well to master it; there is no real difficulty in it, but it requires care and the more evenly it is done, the better it looks, a remark which applies more or less to all knitting.

8. FULL-SIZED WARM PETTICOAT, CROCHET.

Materials required; 1-lb. Petticoat Yarn or Fleecy.

A coarse wooden crochet needle.

Allow 17 stitches for each scallop.

Make a chain of 272 stitches; for convenience of counting put a pin or a piece of white thread at each 50.

Join this long chain in 1 round.

* 7 D.C. (to begin the row make 2 chain instead of the 1st D.C., so that when you come round to it you can join it by a single stitch in 2nd chain: every row must be begun in this way, and when the book says 7 D.C. it means 6 D.C., besides the 2 chain which count for the 1st stitch); 3 D.C. into the 8th chain, 7 D.C., miss 3 chain, repeat from * to end of round; turn the work.

Crochet back in the same way, taking the back loop, so as to make ribbed crochet; continue this till it is sufficiently long, 40 rows or 20 ribs is a good length, fasten off. The last row is the bottom of the petticoat, except the edge, which will be shewn hereafter.

Begin again at the original chain and work round one way and then back again, ribbed crochet, but without any increase or decrease so as to get rid of the scallops.

When this is done and the crochet perfectly straight, the petticoat must be decreased for the waist, and an opening must be left for the placket hole.   This last is very simple, instead of joining the rounds turn back without joining and decrease where necessary by taking 2 together. Some workers make the top of the petticoat in thinner wool—Beehive or Scotch Fingerings, or Berlin Fingering would be very suit-able—crochet along the two edges of the placket hole and put the petticoat into a band, or run in a string.

A child's petticoat may be made in the same way, for which use the Beehive or Scotch Fingerings, or Berlin Fingering, if colours be preferred; if white, either of the vest wools, merino or Lady Betty; a smaller crochet needle.

Allow 13 stitches for each scallop and cast on 199 stitches, the scallop is to be much smaller than in the large petticoat, having 5 D.C. each way instead of 7.

Finish off each petticoat with these fancy rows.

A row of treble stitches round the bottom, miss the 3 centre stitches where they were missed in the previous row, and at the 4 top of the scallop put 1 chain between each of the treble.

2nd row; 1 D.C. on each of the treble, when you come to the chain, put the D.C. in each hole, with 5 chain between each D.C.

9. TRIANGULAR KNITTING.

2 Steel needles, No. 11, Petticoat or Fleecy.
Cast on any number of stitches divisible by 9.
For a strip cast on 27.
1st row ; purl 8, knit 1, repeat.
2nd row ; purl 2, knit 7, repeat.
3rd row ; purl 6, knit 3, repeat.
4th row ; purl 4, knit 5, repeat.
5th row ; purl 4, knit 5, repeat.

6th row ; purl 6, knit 3, repeat.

7th row ; purl 2, knit 7, repeat.

8th and 9th like 1st row, repeat from 2nd row.

10. CABLE KNITTING.

Fleecy or Petticoat Yarn, 3 steel needles, No. 11 ; this makes a very pretty stripe to employ alternately with a stripe of plain, ribbed, or brioche knitting.

Cast on 18 stitches, which gives 6 stitches on each side of the cable.

1st row purl 6, knit 6, purl 6.

2nd row, knit 6, purl 6, knit 6.

3rd and 4th, like 1st and 2nd.

5th like 3rd.

6th, knit 6, take the 3rd needle and purl 3 ; with the first right hand needle purl the next 3 stitches and knit 6.

7th, purl 6, knit the 3 stitches on the additional needle, knit the 3 on the left-hand needle, purl 6.

8th row, like 2nd row ; repeat from 1st row.

11. TO USE UP SCRAPS.

It often happens that knitters have a quantity of wool of various sorts and colours that they don't know what to do with. A very effective coverlet or sofa blanket can be made by knitting the various wools into squares ; join these squares into strips, having regard to assortment of colours and kind, narrow strips of black or navy, or any *one* colour most convenient. If you have to *buy* the wool, black is the most effective ; fine wools, such as Shetlands and Andalusians, can be knitted double. Of course the squares must all be the same size and quite even. The narrow stripes of one colour are sewn between the strips of squares. Finish with a fringe at the two ends.

CHAPTER IV.

BERLIN FINGERING.

This is, comparatively, a wool of recent date, it is beautifully soft, there are a variety of shades and it is exactly adapted for all those purposes requiring softness and lightness without great strength.

I have heard complaints that this wool is more liable to shrink than other kinds, but on inquiring into the matter I have invariably found that the fault lay in the washing, if the instructions for washing woollen articles given at the end of this book, be carried out, the Berlin Fingering will be found eminently satisfactory.

12. CHILD'S SCARF in Double Knitting.

Materials, 4oz. Berlin Fingering or shawl wool— 2 bone needles, No. 8.

Cast on 24 stitches and knit one plain row, slip the 1st stitch every row.

2nd row, 2 plain, * wool in front of the needle slip 1, wool back, knit 1, repeat from * till there are only 3 stitches left on the needle, which must be invariably knitted. Full instructions for double knitting will be found in Chap. iii. (Bassinet blanket). When the scarf is long enough knit a plain row, cast off, and finish the ends with fringe of the same wool.

13. LONG SOCKS for Infants out-of-door wear.

2oz. Berlin Fingering ; 4 short steel needles, No. 14, these are knitted on 2 needles, the extra needles are required for the foot.

In the leg fancy knitting is required 6 rows to the pattern, which is done as follows :

1st row plain.
2nd ,, purl.
3rd ,, 1 plain, 1 purl to end of row.
4th ,, purl.
5th ,, plain.
6th ,, 1 purl 1 plain to end of row.

In the 6th row be careful to purl the stitch which had been knitted plain in the 3rd row.

Cast on 60 stitches.

Rib in twos from 30 rows.

Knit 18 rows of the fancy knitting ; decrease by taking 2 stitches together at the beginning and end of 11th, 13th, 15th, and 18th, fancy rows.

There should be 52 stitches on the needle.

Then begin for the shoe.

Knit 19 stitches and leave them ; take another needle and knit 14 stitches, leaving 19 stitches on the 3rd needle.

Take the 4th needle and knit backwards and forwards on the 14 stitches for 6 fancy rows to form the instep, then knit 22 plain rows, leave off with the wool at the end of the 14 stitches, knit along the flap picking up 23 stitches and then along the last 19 stitches ; turn back, knit along the side of the shoe 41 stitches in all, then the 14 across the end, then pick up 22 along the side, but they must be purled or it will come wrong. Then knit the 19 stitches which had been left on the 1st needle when the foot was begun; there should now be 4 needles in use, the 1st with 41 stitches, the 2nd with 14, the 3rd with 41, the 4th needle to knit with.

Knit 5 plain rows backwards and forwards on the 3 needles.

6th row: decrease by knitting 2 together in the centre of the toe.

Henceforth in every alternate row knit the 3 centre stitches together. When there are 11 ridges or 22 rows done, counting from the commencement of the foot, decrease at the end of every row by taking together the two stitches immediately before the last. When 26 rows, or 13 ridges, are done, cast off at the sole of the foot on the wrong side, taking both edges together, sow up the leg.

14. BABY'S' SHOES.

1½oz. Berlin Fingering; 4 steel needles, No. 14, or No. 15 if a loose knitter.

These are knitted on 2 needles; the 2 extra needles are required for the foot.

Cast on 56 stitches and rib in twos for 24 rows.

Then make a row of holes by putting the wool forward and knitting 2 together the whole length of the row.

Then 5 more ribbed rows.

For the foot; knit 21 plain stitches and leave them. Take another needle and knit 14 plain stitches on the 3rd needle and knit the 14 stitches backwards and forwards for 22 rows—these may be done in fancy knitting by purling and knitting each stitch alternately, care being taken to purl in one row the stitch which was knitted in the previous row so as to give the work somewhat the appearance of little squares. Leave off with the wool at the end of the flap. Pick up (knitted) 17 stitches along the side of the flap, and then knit the 21 stitches which were left on the 3rd needle, making 38 in all ; turn.

Knit back to the end of the needle.

Knit the 14 stitches at the toe, pick up 17 stitches along the side of the flap, only they must be purled instead of knitted.   Knit the 21 stitches which were left on the 1st needle—there should now be 4 needles in use—the 1st or side needle with 38 stitches, the 2nd or toe needle with 14 stitches, the 3rd or side needle with 38, the 4th to knit with.

Knit 5 plain rows backwards and forwards on the 3 needles. 6th row, decrease by knitting 3 together in the centre of the toe needle.

Henceforth in every alternate row knit the 3 centre stitches together.

When 9 ridges or 18 rows are done, counting from the commencement of the foot, decrease at the end of every row (the heel part) by taking together the 2 stitches immediately before the last.   When 11 or 12 ridges (22 or 24 rows) are done, cast off on the wrong side—to do this, put the two side needles parallel with each other, knit together a stitch from each needle and cast off at the same time—the stitches on the toe needle will have been absorbed into the reductions.

Sew up the back of the leg, insert ribbon into the holes.

This recipe is in many respects similar to the foot of the previous one—it will be found a very good serviceable shoe, and if worked in the Scotch Fingerings is very strong to give to the poor.

15.   INFANT'S (Boy) HAT.

2 ozs. Berlin Fingering or 4-ply Lady Betty, white. A coarse steel crochet needle and two bone knitting needles, No. 8.

Make a loop of wool and work 3 chain and 16 treble into the loop, draw it tight and join the last treble to the 3rd chain so as to complete the round.

2nd round, * 2 D.C. in the 1st stitch, 1 in the next, repeat from * to end of round.

3rd round, double crochet, increase in every 3rd stitch.

4th round, increase in every 4th stitch.

5th round,   ,,   ,,   5th   ,,

Continue for 15 rounds, in each round there is one more plain stitch between the increasing than in the previous round, this forms the crown of the hat and may be made smaller or larger as circumstances may require.

For the brim or band (knitted).

Cast on 11 stitches and knit a plain row.

2nd row ; slip 1, insert the right hand needle into the next stitch, loop the wool twice over the forefinger of the left hand and knit them (see Child's Muff, chapter V.), make these loops for 9 consecutive stitches altogether, knit the last stitch plain.

3rd row ; plain.

Contine these two rows alternately till the brim is long enough for the crown ; cast off, sew the two ends together and crochet the brim on to the crown on the wrong side.

Line the hat with sarsenet and put strings, make rosettes with wool for the ears in the same way as the brim, with 5 stitches, i.e. 3 loops. When the piece is long enough cast off and make into rosettes.

16. LADY'S MITTENS.

Materials required, 1½oz. Berlin Fingering or 4-ply Sicilian or Dame, or No. 6 German Fingering, or Worcester, or Beehive ; 4 steel needles, No. 15.

These are knitted on 2 needles up and down the hand, the extra needles are required for the thumbs and for knitting borders afterwards at the wrist and top. These are the size for a hand which wears 6½ or 6¾ gloves, for larger mitten use No. 14 needles.

Cast on 50 stitches and knit 2 plain rows and 2 purled rows for 104 rows ; the work will be in small ribs.

When the 104 rows are complete commence the thumb. While knitting this, care must be taken to continue the ribs ; the word knitting will be employed for convenience sake, but it must be understood to mean purl when the ribs require it.

Knit or (purl) 15 stitches and leave them.

Take another needle and with it cast 15 stitches on to the 1st needle.

Knit these 15 and 25 more (leaving 10 on the needle which are to be untouched at present). These 10 are at the wrist, the 35 stitches are for the thumb, and the 15 for the top of the hand. We now work backwards and forwards with 2 needles on these 35 stitches, decreasing at the end of every alternate row by taking two together immediately before the last stitch, the intermediate row is quite plain.

Observe that the top of the thumb must be perfectly straight, the bottom of the thumb slanting, and the decreasings must therefore come at that part of the thumb which is nearest to the wrist. Continue these two rows till there are only 11 stitches instead of 35, and leave off with the wool at the top of the thumb.

Cast off 15 stitches and pick up 24 stitches along the slanting edge of the thumb, and work to the end of the wrist needle which has been untouched all this time. Work back these 35 stitches and take on the 15 stitches which have also been idle ; there should now be 50 stitches and only the two original needles

in use, continue for 10 more rows or 5 ribs and cast
off.   This mitten is for the right hand.

For the left mitton proceed in exactly the same way
till the thumb is finished, then in picking up the 25
stitches along the slanting edge of the thumb, purl
them instead of knitting them, and turn the mitten
the other side out ; finish the ribs (10 more rows).
Cast off.

When both are finished sew them up for right and
left hand on the wrong side ; thumbs also.

Turn them back to the right side and for the top
of the hand pick up 63 stitches, i.e., 21 on each of 3
needles and knit a round, and purl a round alternately
for 12 rounds, i.e., 6 plain rounds and 6 purl rounds.
Cast off and join the wool neatly, the same border
for the thumb, where 30 stitches must be picked up,
10 on each needle.

For the wrist, pick up 62 stitches in the same way,
but they must be ribbed, 1 plain stitch and 1 purl
stitch for 20 rounds or more if a longer mitten be
required.

For thicker mittens 6 ply Scotch Fingering or 6 ply
Sicilian will be found most suitable.   No. 14 needles.

CHAPTER V.

17. LADY'S VEST.

5oz. 4-ply Vest or Lady Betty (for summer wear 3-ply), 2 long wooden needles, No. 8.

Cast on loosely 82 stitches.

1st and 2nd rows plain.

3rd row : slip 1, knit 1, * wool forward, knit 2 together, repeat from * to end of row, knitting the last two stitches plain.

Knit three plain rows ; this is the bottom of the vest, and is the border.

Rib in twos for 23 inches for the body of vest (front) continue the ribbing of the 1st 22 stitches for 5 inches for the 1st shoulder.

Cast off loosely the middle 38 stitches and knit the 2nd shoulder to match the 1st.

Cast on 38 stitches to unite the two shoulders. Continue the ribbing of the whole 82 stitches for 23 inches.

Knit the border as at the beginning to match exactly ; cast off on the right side.

Sleeves : on each side take up the 48 middle stitches and knit a plain row, and knit backwards and forwards, leaving the stitches to be joined under the arm afterwards, 1 purl row and 2 plain rows— repeat these 3 rows for 3 inches, then rib in twos for 2 inches, cast off, sew up the seams with the same wool, beginning from the sleeve, and going down to the bottom of the vest on the wrong side, and fasten off the ends securely. A crochet border round the neck is a great improvement, thus, 3 treble 2 chain, miss 2, repeat.

2nd row, * 1 D.C. in the 2nd of the 3 treble of
last row, 2 treble, 3 chain and 2 treble in 2 chain of
last row, repeat from * and fasten off.

18.   VEST FOR A CHILD (4 or 5 Years).

2½oz. 3-ply Vest wool or Lady Betty; wooden
needles, No. 8.

Cast on 69 stitches; slip 1st stitch of every row.

1st row: knit 12, rib in 3 to within 12 stitches
of end of row, knit these plain.

Continue for 90 rows.

For 1st shoulder, knit the 12 plain stitches for 36
rows.

Cast off loosely the 45 stitches immediately after
the shoulder, and knit the remaining 12 stitches for
36 rows for the other shoulder.

Cast on 45 stitches between the two shoulders and
knit the whole 69 stitches in ribs to match the other
side of the vest for 90 rows.

Cast off, sew up the sides neatly and carefully stitch
by stitch on the wrong side leaving armholes.   Round
the neck and armholes put a narrow crochet edge, thus,
* 1 D.C., 2 chain, miss 1 stitch of the knitting,
repeat from *

2nd row—4 treble into chain of last row. * 1
single into next chain, 4 treble in next, repeat from
* fasten off.

19.   INFANTS VEST.

2 ozs. Lady Betty or Vest Wool, 3-ply; 3 bone
needles, No. 10.

Unlike the two preceding vests, this little garment
is knitted up and down instead of across, it is very
pretty, simple and satisfactory in every way.   If
intended for hospitals or very hard wear, the Beehive

Knitting Yarn or Scotch Fingering is recomnended for this and the preceding patterns. The sizes may be increased by using thicker wool and larger needles.

Cast on one needle 100 stitches.

Knit 3 ribs, i.e., 2 plain rows, 2 purl, 2 plain, the whole length.

Then knit 40 stitches and work upon them with the 3rd needle until you have 22 ribs and leave them. Cast off with the 3rd needle 20 stitches for the shoulder, i.e., the 20 centre stitches of the original hundred, so that there are 40 left, rib these 40 in the same way to match the front for 22 ribs.

In the 43rd row cast on 20 stitches for the other shoulder and join them to the 40 stitches at the front, making the original 100 stitches again, rib these as at the beginning for 6 rows, cast off, sew up the sides leaving the armholes open; make a narrow crochet edge round neck and armholes; 1 single, 2 chain, miss stitch next, repeat to end of row.

2 row * 1 D.C. in chain of last row, 3 chain, 1 D.C. in next 2 chain; 3 chain; repeat from * fasten off neatly.

20. CHILD'S MUFF.

½-lb. Lady Betty, 4 ply or Eider, 2 bone or wooden needles, No. 8.

Cast on 40 stitches and knit a plain row.

2nd row; knit 4 plain, insert the right hand needle in the 3rd stitch, make 3 loops over the 1st finger of left hand, and knit them into the stitch (see boy's hat, Chapter IV.), continue these loops in every stitch till there are only 4 stitches left on the needle, which are to be knitted plain.

3rd row, knit back plain.

Repeat these two rows till the muff is the right

size, cast off, lay the knitting out flat and cut a piece of wadding the size, also a piece of white silk, tack those together and bind the edges where the hands will come with narrow sarsenet ribbon leaving an inch at the beginning and end. Turn the muff the wrong side, join the knitting very carefully at the cast on and cast off edges, and then the wadding and silk, and lastly the inch of ribbon which was left at the edge. Turn the muff, run in wider ribbon and draw up the muff at each end, leaving bows and ends. This muff is exceedingly pretty, very uncommon, and a most attractive article for a bazaar, it must however, be kept spotlessly clean while working.

21. BABY'S HOOD, Very Simple.

2oz. Berlin Fingering, 2 pairs wooden or bone needles, No. 8.

For the crown : cast on 25 stitches, slip 1st stitch of every row. Knit backwards and forwards till you have a square—leave off with wool at right hand corner, cut it, leaving 3 or 4 inches.

Pick up 25 stitches along side of crown, beginning where you cast on. Take another needle and knit along the 25 stitches at top of crown, knitting in the end of wool. Pick up 25 along other side of crown. There should be 75 stitches in all. Knit backwards and forwards along those 75 stitches for 6 inches, cast off—fold the brim back, and tack it along. For the curtain pick up 75 stitches along the back, keeping the brim folded. Knit 1 plain row, then a row of holes, after which knit the curtain 3 inches deep. Increase constantly, in every alternate row, to give the necessary fulness.

Run ribbon through the holes, allow sufficient to tie.

22. BABY'S HOOD.

2oz., 4-ply Eider or Lady Betty, 3 steel needles, No. 10.

Cast on 75 stitches, and knit 36 rows in brioche stitch throughout.

Then knit 50 stitches and turn.

Knit back 24, and with 25th stitch take a stitch off the other needle, turn.

Knit backwards and forwards on these 25 stitches, knitting the 25th stitch into the 1st stitch of next needle, every row till all the stitches are worked off both needles, and there are only the 25 centre stitches left on needle.

Pick up 21 stitches along each side, and knit 12 rows for the curtain, cast off loosely.

Fold the brim back, and sew on a ruche exactly like the band for baby boy's hat, chap. iv., only cast on 7 stitches instead of 11. The ruche may be made in Shetland Wool if preferred, in which case 9 stitches must be cast on and the loops put 7 times round the finger instead of 3 times.

Insert the ribbon through the top of curtain to tie.

This hood may be made in Petticoat Yarn and without the ruche.

To use up small quantities of wool the brim and curtain might be coloured, and the crown white or grey.

23. GLOVES.

Ladies' size : 2oz. Sicilian 4-ply, or Dame, or Rutland, or Scotch Fingering No. 4½, 6 short steel needles No. 15.

Cast on 20 stitches on each of 3 needles, 60 in all. 2 plain and 2 purl for 30 rounds, or if a longer wrist be required 40 or even 50 rounds will not be too much.

For the hand 18 plain rounds.

To increase for the thumb: to increase knit and purl a stitch (2 stitches together) in the same loop, to be done in every third round thus—

19th round increase in 2nd stitch and in 4th.

20th and 21st plain.

22nd increase in 2nd stitch and 5th.

2 plain rounds.

Continue to increase in every 3rd round thus: in the 2nd stitch always. The 2nd increase is to be placed 1 stitch further than the previous increase, till you have 16 extra stitches on the 1st needle, 8 increasings altogether. Knit 18 stitches from the 1st needle, cast on 4. These 22 stitches, which should all be on the same needle, are for the thumb; divide them on three needles, knit round and round on those 22 stitches for 33 rounds. decrease in 34th round thus, 2 together, 1 plain, 35th round plain, 36th plain, 37th decrease as before. 1 plain round, take out your knitting needles, break off your wool about 9 inches, and with a wool needle draw the stitches together neatly and fasten off securely.

Now go on with the hand. Pick up 4 stitches, at the edge of the 4 stitches cast on at the thumb. Knit 20 stitches from the 1st needle, 18 with the 2nd, 20 with the 3rd; knit 2 of the thumb stitches on to the 3rd needle, so that there are 22 on 1st and 3rd needles, quite even on each side of the glove. Knit 27 plain rounds.

To begin the fingers: 1st finger knit 9 stitches from the first needle, cast on 4 stitches, knit off 9 from 3rd needle, arrange these 22 stitches on 3 needles, and knit round and round as before for 36 rounds. Then decrease and finish off as for the thumb.

For the 2nd finger: Pick up 4 stitches along the

4 cast on for 1st finger. Knit 7 from 1st needle,
cast on 4 ; knit 7 from 3rd needle, arrange these 22
on 3 needles as before, knit round and round for 40
rounds, decrease and finish off as before.

For the 3rd finger : pick up 3 stitches from the
cast on edge of 2nd finger, knit 7, cast on 3 stitches,
knit 7. Arrange these 20 on 3 needles. Knit round
and round as before for 36 rounds, decrease and
fasten off.

For the 4th finger : there should be 16 stitches
left. Pick up 2 on the cast on side of 3rd finger,
knit the 16, divide these 18, and knit round and
round as before for 30 rounds, decrease and finish off.

Turn the glove on the wrong side, and fasten off
all ends of wool neatly. . Both gloves are knitted the
same. When the pair is finished fold the thumbs in,
and tack them at the wrist and the top of 2nd finger, .
with thumbs together, press them under a heavy
weight. They will be perfectly satisfactory as right
and left.

Gloves are not at all difficult if the directions are
carefully followed. Fancy gloves are often preferred.
They are made in the same way, except that after
the wrist is finished you purl every alternate stitch
in every 3rd row. You must be careful that the
purled stitch always comes exactly over the previous
one, with 2 plain rounds between.

The same instructions are suitable for gentlemen's
gloves, in thicker wool, 6-ply Sicilian, or Scotch
fingering No. 3. Needles 13 or 14.

These gloves are very serviceable, and new thumb
and fingers can always be knitted in when required.

24. SHOULDER CAPE.
Knitting.
Shawl Wool, or Single Berlin, or German Finger-

ing, or if greater warmth be required, Giant Zephyr, or Zephyr Fleecy, or Ex super Fleecy, or Petticoat may be used. Ostrich would look well but not much warmth. It would, however, be quite suitable if an ornamental wrap only were required. 1 pair long wooden needles No. 7. 2 colours. Of the lighter kinds of wool 6oz. will be sufficient, of the heavier 8 to 10oz. will be required.

Knit loosely, cast on 44 stitches, and knit a plain row. Henceforth slip 1st stitch of each row.

1st row : knit 4 stitches, * wool over needle, knit 4, repeat from *

2nd row : purl 4, * slip off the wool which is over the needle, wool over, purl 4, repeat from * 6 rows in one colour, 6 rows in the other. Be careful that each stripe is reversed, one stripe must look as if knitted throughout, the next as if purled. This gives a fluted appearance to the cape which is very pretty. Knit 59 stripes or any odd number. You must finish with the same colour with which you began. Before casting off, knit or purl, as may be necessary, a row without putting the wool over the needle, cast off 44 stitches, the same number that you cast on.

For the neck : pick up two stitches in the centre of each stripe. Knit a plain row.

2nd row : 2 plain, * wool twice round needle 2 together, repeat from * finish with 2 plain.

3rd row : 2 together, knit one stitch where the wool has been put *twice* round needle. This is to make as large a hole as possible. Knit 6 rows backwards and forwards. Cast off, fasten off ends neatly, and run in the holes at neck ribbon to tie.

CHAPTER VI.

ANDALUSIAN and SHETLAND.

These wools are very fine, very soft and light, consequently there is a very large quantity for the weight. The colours are beautiful and in great variety.

25. VERY FINE BABY SHOES.

Materials required : 1oz. Andalusian White, ½oz. coloured, 1yd. narrow white or coloured ribbon, 4 steel needles No. 16, a coarse steel crochet needle.

These shoes are knitted on 4 needles.

Cast on 20 stitches on 3 needles, 60 in all.

Rib in twos for 20 rounds.

21st round : * wool forward, knit 2 together, repeat from * to end of round—this is to form holes for the ribbon.

6 more ribbed rounds. This finishes the leg.

For the heel : knit to end of 1st needle, turn, purl back these 20 stitches, and 20 more from the 3rd needle, leave the centre or 2nd needle alone for the present.

Knit and purl backwards and forwards these 2 needles for 20 rows, taking care to slip the 1st stitch of every row.

21st heel row—knit 15, knit 2 together, 2 plain, 2 together, 2 plain, 2 together, plain to the end, 15 stitches.

22nd heel row—purl the whole row.

23rd   ,,   knit 13, 2 together, 7 plain, 2 together, plain to the end, 13.

24th   ,,   purl the row.

25th   ,,   knit 11, 2 together, 9 plain, 2 together, plain to end, 11 stitches.

26th   ,,   purl.

27th   ,,   knit 9, 2 together, 11 plain, 2 together turn.

28th   ,,   knit 12, 2 together turn.

Repeat this last row, till all the stitches are taken off on each side and only 13 stitches left on the needle ; leave off with the wool on the wrong side of the work.

Pick up 14 stitches along the edge of the 20 rows, which were knitted backwards and forwards.

Knit along the 2nd needle the 20 stitches which have been so long untouched. Pick up 14 along the other side and knit 7 of the 13 heel stitches on to the 3rd needle. This completes the heel. There should be 20 on the 1st needle, 20 on the 2nd, 21 on the 3rd, 61 altogether. The odd stitch comes in the centre of the sole, and is. henceforth, the seam stitch, to be knitted and purled alternately.

For the foot 20 plain rounds, keeping the seam. After 6 rounds, the front needle is to be fancy knitting; 2 plain, * wool forward 2 together, repeat from *, knit the 2 last stitches on the needle.

2 plain rounds. The holes should come alternately, so in the 2nd row of holes, knit 3 plain stitches at the beginning and end ; in the 3rd row of holes, knit 2 plain, and so on alternately 2 and 3 stitches at the beginning and end of each rows of holes, till the decreasing in the foot are begun, then gradually narrow the fancy knitting to the shape of the foot.

When the 20 rounds are finished, decrease in sole of foot, thus : 1st needle knit 10 plain, slip 1, knit 2 together, pass the slipped stitch over the 2 together, plain to end of needle. 2nd needle without reduction. 3rd needle 7 plain, decrease as before, 10 plain, seam stitch. It will be perceived that each reduction is 2 stitches, making 4 stitches less in that round.

4 plain rounds ; (front needle fancy.)

2nd reduction ; 2 plain, reduce as before, knit to within 12 of seam, decrease in the same way, 9 plain, seam stitch.

4 plain rounds.

3rd reduction as before, but 8 plain stitches each side of the seam.

3 plain rounds.

Continue these reductions, putting them 1 stitch nearer the seam each time, and 3 plain rounds between till there are 7 reductions on each side ; then slip 4 stitches off each end of front needle, on to the 2 back needles leaving 12 stitches, which must, of course, be the 12 centre stitches.

Continue the reductions, 2 more will be required, having 4 plain stitches each side of the seam, 3 plain rows after each. There should be 25 stitches altogether, 12 on front, and 13 on the back, turn the sock inside out and put all the back stitches on one needle, cast off on the wrong side by putting the needles parallel, and knitting one off each needle together—the 6th and 7th stitches of the back needle must be knitted as one, fasten off ends, and turn the sock right side out.

For the crochet trimming.

With the coloured wool, make a D.C. stitch in one of the knitted ribs at the top of the leg—5 ch. D.C. in the next knitted rib 5 ch. continue to end of round, there should be 15 loops of 5 ch. altogether, fasten off and cut the wool.

Do the same in the purled ribs, and fasten off the

wool, there should now be two distinct rounds of
crochet, separate from each other in top of leg, the
1st round is to be left to itself.

In the 2nd round, with the white wool 1 D.C. in a
5ch. of 2nd round, * 6 ch. D.C. in same loop, 4 ch.
D.C. in next loop, repeat from * to end of round,
fasten off.

4th, coloured wool; 1 D.C. in loop of 6 ch., * 5
ch. D.C. in same loop, 5 ch. D.C. in loop of 4 ch., 5
ch. D.C. in loop of 6 ch., repeat from * to end of
round.

With the coloured wool sew the points of the
scallops along the ribs, just above the row of holes.
In these holes place narrow ribbon, white or coloured.

If these shoes are for a bazaar, they should be tied
together at the tops, and their appearance will be
greatly improved by putting cardboard soles in the
foot, and a roll of white paper in the legs to keep the
shape. These shoes are generally much admired, they
wash well, and keep their shape to the last. They
can be made entirely in white if preferred, and in this
case, the first crochet row, should be Filoselle silk, 6
threads, and the points sewn down with silk.

26. SHAWLS (Crochet.)

Materials required : Shetland, Andalusian, Lady
Betty, Pyrenees, or Berlin Fingering, a very coarse
wooden crochet needle.

The above-mentioned wools are all suitable for this
shawl, and should be used at the discretion of the
worker. Shetland is the thinest, Berlin Fingering the
thickest. Of the Shetland, 6 ozs. will be required for
a good sized shawl, of the others from 8 ozs. to 10 ozs.,
it must be worked loose.

Make a loop of wool and work into it 8 treble.

These shawls should be perfectly square and to keep
the shape it is very necessary to finish each row before
beginning the next. On no account work round and
round, therefore make 3 chain for the 1st treble, and
at the end of the round join with a single stitch into
the 3rd of these chain, do this at the beginning and
end of every round.

2nd round, 2 treble between each treble of 1st
round, 16 stitches in all, join as already
directed.

3rd round, 2 treble between 1st and 2nd stitch of
2nd round, 2 chain, 2 treble between next
2 stitches; continue to end of round;
complete as before.

4th round, make 1 ch. and insert needle into loop
made by 2 chain in previous round, * 2
treble (bear in mind that the 1st treble
of every round is always to be 3 chain) 3
ch., 2 treble, all in the same loop, 1 ch.,
2 treble between next 2 treble of previous
row, 2 ch., 2 treble in next, 2 treble ch.,
2 treble in the same space, 3 ch., 2 treble
in next 2 treble, 2 chain, which should
bring you to the 2nd corner, repeat from
* and complete round as before.

5th round, 2 treble, 3 ch., 2 treble at corner, 2 ch.,
2 treble, 3 chain, 2 treble in next, 2
treble, 2 chain, repeat to end of round.
This is the beginning of shawl, it should
be perfectly square; the remainder is
quite easy.

2 treble, 3 ch., 2 treble in every 3 chain of previous,
2 ch. ; to increase, do the corner thus : 2 treble, 3
ch., 2 treble, 3 ch., 2 treble, 3 ch., 2 treble, all in the
corner ; these increasings will not be required in
every row. The finer the wool and the coarser the
needle, the more lacey the shawl will look.

27. THREE-CORNERED SHAWL FOR SHOULDERS.

¾lb. Fleecy or 10ozs. Petticoat Yarn, or 8ozs. Scotch
Fingering, a large wooden or bone crochet needle,
rather finer for the Fingering than for the other
wools. 4 chain, 2 treble in 1st stitch, 3 chain, 3
treble in same as before; turn.

2nd row, 3 chain 2 treble in last stitch of previous
row. 3 treble in space between the 3 treble; go on
backwards and forwards till your shawl is large enough,
taking care that at the centre of each row you put
3 treble, 3 chain, 3 treble in space made by 3 chain
of previous row.

Crochet along the slanting, edge to strengthen it
if preferred, 2 colours can be used, black with a
crimson border, and other mixtures.

It may be finished off with a row of D C.
along the two slanting sides and the neck, and a
fringe put at the edge. For the fringe, wind the
wool loosely round the short way of a post card, and
cut it, take 4 or 5 strands, fold the ends together,
draw the centre through the alternate spaces of the
3 treble, and pass the ends through it, and draw
them tight. It should be done on the wrong side of
the work.

28. KNITTED SHAWL, One Yard Square.

1lb. Single Berlin, or Andalusian, or the New
Crochet Wool, or Shetland, or Madras; 1 pair very
long wooden needles, No. 4.

Cast 152 stitches, or any number divisible by 4.
Knit loosely but evenly, slip 1st stitch throughout.

Knit 1 plain row, after which—

1st row: slip 1, knit 1, * make 3 stitches in next

thus, knit 1, purl 1, knit 1, all in
same stitch, purl the next 3 together,
repeat from * till there are only 2 stitches
left on needle, knit these plain

2nd row : slip 1, knit 1, purl the remainder, except
the last 2, which must be knitted.

3rd row : slip 1, knit 1, * purl 3 together, knit 1,
purl 1, knit 1 in the same stitch, repeat
from * last 2 stitches plain.

4th row : slip 1, knit 1, purl entire row, except 2
last, which are to be plain.

Repeat these 4 rows till the shawl is quite square,
knit a plain row and cast off. May be finished off
with fringe.

29. CLOUD, Knitted.

1lb. Coral Wool, or Madras, long wooden needles
No. 4.

Cast on 100 stitches and knit a plain row.

1st row : slip 1, knit 1, * wool twice round needle,
knit two together, repeat from * till there
are 3 stitches left, which are to be plain.

2nd row : plain, making 1 stitch only where the
wool was twice over the needle (worked
thus to make larger holes).

3rd and 4th rows : plain.

Repeat these 4 rows till the cloud is long enough,
cast off, draw the ends together, and make good full
tassels.

CHAPTER VII.

KNITTING IN ELEMENTARY SCHOOLS AND FOR THE POOR.

Since the Education Act of 1870, the art of knitting has made enormous progress among the working classes. Previous to that time it was almost unknown in England, Scotland and Wales seeming to have a proprietary right in it; and while it was a matter of course that the Scotch Fishwife and the Welsh Dairymaid should always be knitting, the English-woman's fingers were idle, at those times, such as going to market, or taking a journey, when she might have been at work.

It will, I fear, be a long time before we see the English woman take out her knitting in the train, or knit as she walks along the road as the Scotch and Welsh have done for years; but we shall, I hope, arrive at that result in time.

Knitting is now taught in all Elementary Schools as part of the Education Scheme, there is no option, it is *compulsory* for girls and is recommended for boys.

Having had a large experience in schools, I have no hesitation in saying that knitting is a very important aid in teaching the art of needlework generally. I am sorry to say that the time allowed now-a-days for needlework in Elementary Schools is far too short. There is an immense deal to learn, a great deal of which requires patient industry and manual dexterity, only to be acquired by constant practice.

There can be no doubt that to every woman, but most thoroughly and especially to a poor woman, needlework is of the utmost importance. With this view, some people think that knitting in schools is useless, as compared with other work; it is a great deal of trouble at first, the managers grudge the time spent upon it, would abolish it altogether if it were not for the "code" and it is very often so badly taught in consequence that it really is useless and the time spent upon it as a matter of fact, wasted. There cannot be a greater mistake. Let the children be taught thoroughly, they always like it, and will soon learn to take it up if they are waiting for their other work, and it gives a dexterity of finger and correctness of eye which are invaluable afterwards.

The habit of taking up the knitting at odd moments is, of itself, worth a great deal, and from every point of view I regard good knitting as so valuable that I wish the boys could be taught too, it would do more than anything else towards converting clumsy fingers into dexterous ones, and who can tell how greatly they may afterwards benefit by the possession of a quick touch and correct eye.

It is, however, a great deal of trouble to teach knitting well, especially if there are large numbers to deal with. The needlework afternoon is the hardest part of the teacher's work, i.e., if she be trying conscientiously to do her duty—sometimes she gives up in despair and the girls have to do as they best can (very bad indeed is that best), and instead of liking their work, which is the greatest thing to be desired, they hate it, do as little as possible, and the precious time is worse than wasted.

Here, then, is an unlimited field for usefulness. There are many ladies with abundant leisure who might do a work of real practical usefulness by undertaking the knitting in the village school, or, if the numbers are too great, she might undertake one or two standards. I am sure the mistress would welcome such assistance, and the lady, although she might find it strange at first, would soon learn to take the utmost pleasure in it.

A work of this kind, however, requires certain qualifications. Dilletante efforts are no use. She must be thorough, patient, regular, and, of course, mistress of the art before she can attempt to teach others.

One great difficulty in knitting in schools, is the wool; the managers do not like to spend money on a thing which they do not care about, and for which they have little return, if they do buy any it is the cheapest to be had and as no one is responsible for it, it is, to a great extent, wasted. Nothing could be more unsatisfactory; quite sufficient in itself to make the knitting a failure. If the lady who looks after the knitting would also procure the wool, she will have done much towards success. I do not mean that she is to *give* the wool, for many reasons that would not be advisable, but buy a spindle (6 lbs.) of a good useful wool and let the children have it in small quantities at cost price. The children, of course, do not know what wool to get nor the quantity, and in a country village nothing of the sort is to be had—if they send to the adjacent town they will probably have to pay a high price for a very inferior article, to say nothing of carriage—and supposing they do get the wool, it will only be a small quantity and very likely they would be unable to match it when they wanted more.

I strongly advise all those ladies who want to give real help in the school knitting to get, as the first step, a spindle of Jevon's Scotch Fingering, No. 1 or No. 2, which are all excellent in every respect, which wash well, are very strong, soft, and even, and the price very moderate.

If they can obtain good wool easily the children will buy it, and knit stockings for themselves, they will take pains with them, the parents are delighted, and the chief difficulty at once disappears, the same wool should always be kept in order that it may match, and be ready when wanted. The children should be taught to buy good wool and not allowed to waste their time in knitting rubbish, it should be explained to them that very low priced yarns are heavy, and although the cost per oz. may be actually less, they will require a larger quantity, so that by the time the stockings are finished, they will have cost as much, if not more, and will wear out much sooner than if made with the best wool.

I should not, of course, waste good wool upon beginners; they must be taught with coarse cotton. The cuffs, knitted on 4 needles, as required by the "Code," should be done in coarse wool, but it should be good wool. There is no loss upon these, if well made they will always sell among the children themselves for the price of the wool, an extra 1d. should be charged to cover waste.

When the children have advanced to socks and stockings, it is a good plan to let them make a pair of sleeping socks in White Petticoat Yarn, No. 1 on the Table, with steel needles; No. 12 will make a pair for a lady, 20 ribbed rows instead of 34. With this wool they can see the stitches, and it is not such an undertaking for a child to begin with.

Her pride and delight when she finishes them are unbounded, and she is eager to begin a pair of stockings for herself, or socks for a little brother.

It is almost unnecessary to point out that a strict account of the wool should be kept, the lady should provide herself with a little book, which she should take to the school on the knitting day, and, in the presence of the child, enter all wool that is not paid for at the time, and be very careful to cross out the entry when it is paid for. All this, of course, is a great deal of trouble, but nothing can be done without trouble, and I am convinced that the first element of success is, that the children should be able to get good wool at a moderate price without difficulty.

When it is known that good knitting is done at the school, orders will come in--6 pairs Gentlemen's Socks here, Boy's Knickerbocker Stockings, then Socks and Stockings to be re-footed, &c., &c.

These are, of course, paid for, and must be well done, they must be thoroughly looked after by the lady ; part of the money is given to the girl who knits them. All this is a great deal of trouble to the lady, of course, but for all that she should welcome " orders," the children are delighted with the money, they will take their knitting home and go on with it at every available moment, and the hope of an " order " being allotted to them is a very powerful incentive to knit well.

The lady should, in school, wear an apron with pockets, and carry a pair of scissors and a pencil, extra needles, a crochet needle for picking up stitches, a piece of emery paper in case the needles may have become rusty, and above all, a book for teaching—uniformity of teaching is essential ; it is of no use to teach in a haphazard sort of way, by rule of thumb, or by measure. The lady should adopt one method and keep to it ; explain the book to the children so that they can understand it for themselves, and she will reduce her trouble to a minimum ; and, what is of more importance. the girls will be able to go on a;ter they leave school, and for the rest of their lives.

Knitting needles are provided by the school, but the girls will buy them for themselves if they can get them at 1d. per set; short needles always.

I do not know a more practical field for usefulness than helping with the needlework of a village school, besides the work itself the lady obtains great influence over the girls, she learns their characters more intimately than would otherwise be possible, can recommend them for domestic service, in short her opportunities for doing good thus opened in a sphere peculiarly her own are unbounded.

In concluding this chapter, I would say a few words as to knitting for the poor.

There are many women of means and leisure, who, while feeling themselves unfitted for the active work just described would yet like to employ their spare time for the benefit of their poorer neighbours.

To them, I hope this little book will prove useful, knee-caps, petticoats, baby's hoods &c., are gifts which are dear alike to the heart of the rheumatic old dame, the school girl, the choir boy, the fond mother, &c.

The Vests in Chapter v. are delightful gifts for a children's hospital. Small quantities of different colours may be made into a coloured quilt by knitting them all into squares, (either plain or the triangular knitting of Chapter iii,) of the same size; join in stripes and knit narrow stripes of black, or a colour to go between; sew or knit them together, and use up all small pieces to fringe the ends If there are only small quantities of wool, the squares might be made of two colours, the wool may be different sorts, but all the squares must be the same size.

Scraps may be used for petticoats working them in stripes, wider or narrower, according to the quantity of wool; a very good effect may be produced if the colours be arranged with care and judgment.

CONCLUSION.

A FEW WORDS ABOUT THE KNITTING MACHINE.

A book about knitting, would, in these days be very incomplete without some reference to the knitting machine. It is an admirable invention, perfectly satisfactory in every way, but its present high price prevents its being adopted in ordinary households.

It is very generally used in all large institutions; it has already found its way into some English homes, and a case was brought under my notice, quite recently, of a lady who had made a large sum of money towards building a church, from the profits of her knitting machine. There can be no doubt that the sale would be very large indeed, if they were less expensive, and I fully believe that in the next generation it will be considered quite as much a necessity as the sewing machine is now, and that the better class of servants will be required to use it. With this view the necessity for teaching good knitting in elementary schools becomes of the utmost importance. It cannot be too strongly impressed upon the would-be possessor of a machine that it is absolutely useless to those who are ignorant of the art of knitting. The better and more experienced the knitter, the more useful will be the machine. In *her* hands the machine becomes a faithful obedient slave, always ready for work and performing that work with a rapidity and precision which are truly amazing. The machine does not do fancy knitting, in short, whether we have a machine or not, we shall do well to master all the details of knitting for its own sake. If ever we do find ourselves the happy possessor of this delightful invention, we shall find our knowledge, skill, and experience, more valuable every day.

TO WASH WOOLLEN ARTICLES.

Especially Berlin Fingerings, Merino, Lady Betty, Vest Wool, Andalusian and Shetland.

½lb. soap dissolved, should be used to two gallons of warm water.

It cannot be too strongly impressed upon our readers that water used too hot has a worse effect on wools and dye than even strong soaps. Never use water for washing woollen articles hotter than you can bear your hand in. Water of too high a temperature shrinks the fabric and ruins the colour.

The articles to be washed should be well rinsed in this lather, and drawn repeatedly through the hand, wring them dry to remove the soap, rinse them again briskly, in clean lukewarm water; stretch and wring them to their proper shape, and dry them *quickly*; in the open air if possible.

Rubbing shrinks, and destroys the material, the articles should, therefore, not be rubbed.

Avoid boiling water, and do not let the articles lie about damp.

The wools mentioned in this book are in all cases exactly suited to the purpose for which they are recommended. They are sold by Messrs. Jevons and Mellor, Corporation Street, Birmingham, who supply large or small quantities direct on application.

THE END.

THE MEOPHAM SAMPLER FOR SIMULTANEOUS TEACHING.

A B C D E F G H I J K L M N O P Q R
S T U V W X Y Z -|- 1 2 3 4 5 6 7 8 9 10

a b c d e f g h i j k l m n o p q r s t u v w x y z

Mary Jane Robinson aged 11

MEOPHAM N. SCHOOL

She seeketh wool and flax

and worketh willingly

with her hands.

MARKING must be perfectly NEAT on the WRONG side ; the first stitch is worked from left to right TWICE, and crossed ONCE ; each letter must be fastened off separately. No knots allowed ; to commence, leave an inch of cotton at the back and work it in carefully with the succeeding stitches. For a sample this size, a piece of yellow canvas is required 13 inches by 9½ which allows 1 inch all round for the hem ; blue and red cotton.

To be had of the National Society, Sanctuary, Westminster, S.W.; the Midland Educational Company, Birmingham and Leicester; The Scholastic Trading Company, Manchester and Bristol; The North of England School Furnishing Company, Darlington and Newcastle-on-Tyne; The Scholastic Trading Company, Bridewell Place, E.C.; Northern Educational Trading Company, York and Leeds; and of Mrs. Lewis, Meopham Vicarage, near Gravesend, who also supplies all requisites for School Marking.

JEVONS & MELLOR'S

CELEBRATED

SCOTCH FINGERING WOOLS

IN FIVE QUALITIES.

No. 1.—Middle Scotch Fingering for Charitable Purposes.

No. 2.—Super Scotch Fingering, for use in Schools, and for Stockings for the Deep Sea Fishermen.

No. 3.—Ex Super Scotch Fingering, thoroughly reliable for Medium Hosiery.

No. 4.—Ex. Ex. Super Scotch Fingering, rather thicker, makes grand heavy Men's Stockings.

No. 4½.—Original Scotch Fingering, fine, soft and strong, for Ladies and best Hosiery.

BIRMINGHAM.

BERLIN WOOLS,
SHETLAND WOOL,
ANDALUSIAN WOOL,
PYRENEES WOOL,
EYDER or MERINO WOOL
LADY BETTY WOOL,
FLEECY WOOLS,
PETTICOAT YARN,
VEST WOOLS,
BERLIN FINGERING,
SCOTCH FINGERINGS,
GERMAN FINGERINGS,
WORSTEDS,
WHEELING YARNS,
RUG WOOL.